FRENCH
MIDDLE EASTERN CUISINE

Ashraf Saleh

NEW
HOLLAND

Contents

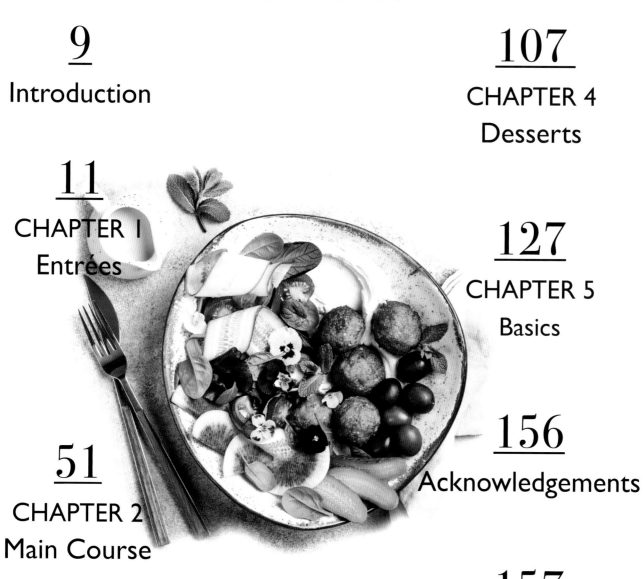

Introduction

During my childhood, whenever I entered my home I found the delicious aromas of appetizing spices wafting through the air. I often helped my mother to prepare fantastic feasts.

I grew up in the Middle East, beginning my career as a chef in the late 1970s. I embarked on a journey through Paris in the early 1980s, then on to London and Sweden in a quest to further refine my culinary expertise.

The mouthwatering tastes of Middle Eastern dishes are often enjoyed on dinner tables all around the world. The popularity of Middle Eastern cuisine can perhaps be attributed to connoisseurs of good taste sampling these delicacies, and then wanting to learn how to recreate it. The serving of Middle Eastern dishes came to signify an important addition to a feast or celebration and a way of welcoming a special guest. In our home, a guest is always welcome and treated as a part of the family around the table.

I simply love to cook! I enjoy cooking at my restaurant for customers and cooking at home for my family. It is extremely rare that I go through a single day without cooking. To me, the kitchen is the core of the home. It brings everyone together, where we can enjoy what we love to eat, talk about the food that we are enjoying, and learning about culture and the history of food — it's one of life's pleasures.

I think about food all the time, especially on my day off. I love to go to the markets, looking for fresh ingredients and produce. I bring them home and get cracking. My family loves everything I make because I keep things simple and work around what is in season. We are blessed with variety and choice, there is always something new and exciting on offer.

My wife and our family have traveled to China where I learnt about Chinese cuisine, their use of spices and basic cooking techniques. This has expanded my knowledge even further.

I use the recipes in this book for my restaurant, Coya, and also at home, with different ways of plating and presenting. They are simple, easy and can be enjoyed anytime, anywhere! Since working as an apprentice, I've always wanted to do things my own way. I consider my food 'Middle Eastern Fusion'. It's about reinventing classics with my personal interpretations.

Ashraf Saleh

Chapter 1

Entrées

Vegetable tartare with avocado fluid gel & rice crisps

(V)
Serves: 4
Time: 30 minutes

1 punnet heirloom cherry tomatoes
1 heirloom red carrot
1 heirloom yellow carrot
1 heirloom purple carrot
½ avocado
1 baby zucchini (courgette), cut in ribbons or rounds
1 handful heirloom purple cauliflower
50 ml (1¾ fl oz) olive oil
zest and juice of 1 lemon
1 tablespoon chives
salt and pepper, to season
rice crisps, to serve
50 g (1 ¾ oz) walnuts, to garnish

Avocado fluid gel
75 g (2½ oz) white sugar
150 ml (5 fl oz) lemon juice
2 g (1/8 oz) xanthan gum
1½ avocados
pinch of salt

Dice the cherry tomatoes, carrots, cauliflower and half an avocado into same size pieces. Mix together with the zucchini and toss gently with the olive oil, lemon, chives and salt and pepper.

To make the avocado fluid gel, boil the sugar and lemon juice until the sugar is dissolved. Add the xanthan gum and boil for 1 minute. Place in a blender with 1 ½ avocados and purée until smooth, then season to taste. Add to a squeeze bottle for serving.

To serve, place a ring mold on the plate and fill with the vegetable mixture. Remove the mold and squeeze the avocado fluid gel on top. Top with a rice crisp and garnish with walnuts.

Fleur de Courgette Farcies
au Fromage
(Zucchini flowers stuffed with cheese)

(V)
Serves: 4
Time: 1 hour

200 g (7 oz) ricotta cheese
20 g (¾ oz) parmesan cheese
40 g (1 ½ oz) gorgonzola cheese
40 g (1 ½ oz) mozzarella cheese
12 zucchini (courgette) flowers
1.5 litres (52 fl oz/6 cups) oil, for frying
100 g (3 ½ oz) baby herbs, to garnish

Batter
200 g (6 ⅔ oz) self-raising (self-rising) flour
300 ml (10½ fl oz) soda water

Saffron emulsion
125 g (4 ½ oz/½ cup) dijon mustard
375 ml (13 fl oz/1 ½ cups) lemon juice
250 ml (9 fl oz/1 cup) vegetable oil
1 teaspoon sugar
a few threads of saffron

Mix the four cheeses together and divide into 12 balls. Trim the ends of the zucchini and remove the stamens from inside the flower. Stuff one portion of the cheese mixture into each flower and gently close.

To make the batter, whisk the flour and soda water together to a smooth consistency.

To make the saffron emulsion, place the mustard, lemon juice, oil, sugar and saffron in a blender. Blend until combined, then transfer to a squeeze bottle to serve.

Dip the flower end of the zucchini in the batter and drain off any excess. Heat the oil in a deep frying pan to 180°C (350°F). Deep fry for 2–3 minutes on each side, then drain off any excess oil on paper towel.

To serve, pour the broth into individual bowls and top with the fried zucchini flowers, Garnish with target beetroot and baby herbs.

Arnabeet

(V)
Serves: 6
Time: 30 minutes

1 litre (35 fl oz/4 cups) oil, for deep-frying
1 large cauliflower, cut into florets
micro coriander (cilantro), to garnish

Dressing
3 garlic cloves, crushed
50 ml (1 ¾ fl oz) olive oil
salt and pepper, to season
pinch of sumac

Tahini sauce
100 g (3 ½ oz) tahini
100 ml (3 ½ fl oz) lemon juice
100 ml (3 ½ fl oz) water
pinch of chili powder
3 garlic cloves, crushed
pinch of cumin
1 teaspoon sea salt

Heat the oil in a deep frying pan to 180°C (350°F). Deep fry the cauliflower for 5–6 minutes, or until golden and soft. Place in a bowl with the dressing ingredients. Mix until combined, then set aside.

To make the tahini sauce, place all of the ingredients in a blender and mix until smooth.

Place the cauliflower in the center of a sharing plate. Drizzle with the tahini sauce and garnish with micro coriander.

Lollipop chicken

Serves: 6
Time: 1½ hours

6 slices white sourdough bread (crusts removed), torn into small pieces
500 ml (17 fl oz/2 cups) chicken stock
50 g (1 ¾ oz) butter
1 tablespoon olive oil
1 small onion, finely diced
3 garlic cloves, crushed
500 g (1 lb 2 oz) minced (ground) chicken
zest and juice of 1 lemon
2 red long chilies, finely chopped
2 tablespoons chopped coriander (cilantro)
salt and pepper, to season

Soak the bread in the chicken stock.

Heat the butter and oil in a frying pan over medium heat. Add the onion and garlic and sauté until translucent. Allow to cool.

Preheat the oven to 160°C (315°F). Line a baking tray with baking paper.

In a large mixing bowl, combine the chicken, onion mixture and remaining ingredients.

Squeeze the excess liquid from the soaked bread and add the bread to the chicken mixture. Mix until well combined, then form into 18 bite-size meatballs.

Place the meatballs on the tray and bake for 20 minutes.

Making the lollipops

100 g (3 ½ oz) cornflour (cornstarch)
4 whole eggs
250 g (9 oz) panko breadcrumbs
oil, for deep-frying

Set up three bowls with the cornflour in the first one, a second bowl with eggs and 2 teaspoons water, beaten together lightly. Put panko crumbs in the third bowl.

Dip the cooked meatballs in the flour, then egg mixture, then the breadcrumbs. Press to coat them well.

Fry the coated meatballs in a deep-fryer at 180°C (350°F) for 2–3 minutes, or until a golden color.

Place the lollipops stick in the center of each meatball. Serve with the sauce.

Sauce

3 teaspoons dijon mustard
1 teaspoon sugar
zest and juice of 2 lemons
a few threads of saffron
100 ml (3 ½ oz) extra virgin olive oil
salt and white pepper

Place all of the ingredients in a blender and blend until combined. Pour into a squeeze bottle for serving.

Moroccan chickpea & tomato soup

Serves: 4
Time: 1 hour, plus overnight soaking

200 g (7 oz) dried chickpeas
100 g (3 ½ oz) butter
1 large onion, peeled and diced
6 garlic cloves, crushed
80 g (2 ¾ oz/½ cup) diced carrot
70 g (2 ½ oz/½ cup) diced celery
80 g (2 ¾ oz/½ cup) diced capsicum
(pepper)
4 bay leaves
125 g (4½ oz/½ cup) tomato paste
(concentrated purée)
500 ml (17 fl oz/2 cups) vegetable stock
1 teaspoon salt
pinch of chili flakes
22 g (¾ oz/½ cup) chopped flat-leaf (Italian)
parsley

Soak the chickpeas in water overnight. The
next day, drain the chickpeas, add 1.5 litres (52
fl oz/6 cups) of water and boil until al dente.
Drain and set aside.

Melt the butter in a saucepan over medium
heat. Add the onion, garlic, carrot, celery
and capsicum and sauté. Add the bay leaves,
tomato paste, vegetable stock and the cooked
chickpeas. Cook until tender.

Serve garnished with chili flakes and parsley

Exotic mushroom soup
with gourmet bread

(V)
Serves: 6
Time: 30 minutes

200 g (7 oz) butter
1 onion, peeled and chopped
4 garlic cloves
a few springs of thyme
1 kg (2 lb 4 oz) mixed mushrooms (button, Swiss brown, king oyster)
½ teaspoon porcini powder
500 ml (17 fl oz/2 cups) vegetable stock
300 ml (10 ½ fl oz/1 ¼ cups) cream
gourmet bread, to serve (See page 150)
salt and pepper, to season

Melt 50 g (1 ¾ oz) of the butter in a saucepan over medium heat. Add the onion, garlic and thyme and sauté. Add the mushrooms and cook until tender, then add the porcini powder. Add the vegetable stock and bring to the boil. Add the cream and remove from the heat. Allow to cool slightly.

Remove the thyme stalks before placing the mushroom mixture in a blender. Blend, then add the remaining 150 g (5½ oz) of the butter and season to taste.

To serve, grill (broil) four pieces of bread on a griddle pan. Pour the soup into large coffee cups or bowls. Serve the bread on the side.

Cauliflower soup with crab croquettes

Serves: 6
Time: 1 hour

Soup

1 large cauliflower, cut into florets
1 litre (35 fl oz/4 cups) milk
500 ml (17 fl oz/2 cups) cream
200 g (7 oz) butter
100 ml (3 ½ oz) vegetable stock
salt and pepper, to season

Croquettes

200 g (7 oz) potatoes, peeled and diced
50 g (1 ¾ oz) crab meat
50 g (1 ¾ oz) butter
60 ml (2 fl oz) cream
4 eggs
2 teaspoons milk
50 g (1 ¾ oz) cornflour (cornstarch)
100 g (3 ½ oz) breadcrumbs
500 ml (17 fl oz/2 cups) oil, for frying

Boil the cauliflower florets in the milk in a saucepan over medium heat for 15 minutes, or until tender. Strain the cauliflower and return to the pot with the cream. Boil until reduced slightly, then allow to cool. Blend until smooth, then add the butter and stock. Season to taste.

Boil the potatoes for 15 minutes, or until tender, then drain and mash.

Mix the crab meat, butter, cream and seasoning with the mashed potatoes. Set aside to cool. When cooled, roll to make 18 croquettes.

Lightly beat the eggs and milk together in a bowl. To crumb the croquettes, roll in the cornflour, then the egg wash mixture and finally in the breadcrumbs. Set aside to firm up.

Heat the oil in a frying pan over high heat and fry the croquettes until crisp and golden. Drain the excess oil on paper towel.

Reheat the soup. To serve, pour the soup into individual bowls and place three croquettes in each bowl. Serve immediately.

Scallops, pork belly and mango salsa

Serves: 4
Time: 25 minutes

pork belly, 4 pieces about 3 cm × 10 cm (1¼ in × 4 in)
20 ml (⅔ fl oz) oil
12 scallops
50 g (1 ¾ oz) butter
lemon cheeks, to garnish
micro coriander (cilantro), to garnish

Mango salsa
1 mango, finely diced
1 tablespoon chopped chives
1 tablespoon chopped red capsicum (pepper)

To make the salsa, combine the mango, chives and capsicum, then set aside.

Sear the pork belly with the oil in a frying pan over medium heat, then set aside for serving.

In the same pan, sear the scallops for 3 minutes, then turn over and cook for a further minute. Turn off the heat. Add the butter to melt and baste the butter over the top of the scallops.

To serve, place a piece of pork belly on the plate and top with 2 scallops. Add the salsa to the side and garnish with a lemon cheek and micro coriander.

Batinjan (fried eggplant) with garlic, lemon, chili, tahini and watermelon radish

(V)
Serves: 4
Time: 20 minutes

8 Japanese or Lebanese eggplant (aubergine)
1 litre (35 fl oz/4 cups) oil
1 lemon
4 garlic cloves
1 long red chili
80 ml (2 ⅔ fl oz) tahini sauce (see page 16)
micro herbs, to garnish
salt and pepper, to season

Peel the eggplant and slice in half lengthways. Heat the oil in a deep frying pan to 180°C (350°F). Deep-fry the eggplant until golden and tender. (For large eggplants, finish cooking in a 180°C (350°F) oven until cooked through.)

Blend the lemon juice, garlic and chili to a paste and pour over the eggplant.

To serve, place the eggplant in the center of a plate and drizzle with the tahini sauce. Top with micro herbs..

Chermoula popcorn chicken with tahini sauce

Serves: 4
Time: 1½ hours

200 g (7 oz) skinless and boneless chicken breast
100 g (3 ½ oz) cornflour (cornstarch)
1 egg, lightly beaten
50 g (1 ¾ oz) popcorn, cooked and crushed
1 litre (35 fl oz/4 cups) oil
tahini sauce (see page 16), to serve

Chermoula

1 tablespoon finely chopped coriander (cilantro)
1 tablespoon finely chopped flat-leaf (Italian) parsley
1 tablespoon finely chopped green capsicum (pepper)
1 tablespoon finely chopped long green chili, de-seeded
1 tablespoon ground cumin
1 tablespoon ground caraway
1 tablespoon fennel seeds
1 tablespoon celery salt
a few threads of saffron

1 tablespoon finely chopped preserved lemon
1 teaspoon crushed garlic
50 ml (1 ¾ fl oz) olive oil

To make the chermoula, add all of the ingredients to a blender and purée. Sauté the mixture slowly in a pan until the oil splits out. Store in a jar topped with oil (this will keep for a few days).

Dice the chicken breast into 5 mm (¼ in) cubes. Marinate with 1 tablespoon of the chermoula spice mix for 1 hour.

Dust the chicken with cornflour, then dip in egg wash and coat in the crushed popcorn. Heat the oil in a deep frying pan to 180°C (350°F). Deep-fry the chicken until golden and crispy, then drain on paper towel.

To serve, dust a plate with crushed popcorn and top with the chicken. Serve with tahini sauce on the side in a small ramekin.

Heirloom baby carrots chargrilled with tahini, lemon, chili & hint of honey

Serves: 6
Time: 20 minutes

4 bunches baby carrots (yellow, red, orange, white), peeled and trimmed
2 garlic cloves, crushed
1 tablespoon olive oil
salt and pepper, to season
1 lemon, to serve
baby parsley, to garnish

Tahini

125 ml (4 fl oz/½ cup) lemon juice
4 garlic cloves
½ teaspoon cumin
¼ teaspoon chili powder
1 teaspoon honey
1 teaspoon salt
50 ml (1 ¾ fl oz) water

Blanch the carrots in boiling water, then place in ice water to refresh. Drain and mix with the garlic, olive oil and salt and pepper. Chargrill the carrots, then transfer to a serving platter.

To make the tahini, combine all of the ingredients in a blender and mix until combined.

To serve, place the carrots on a serving platter and drizzle with the tahini dressing. Finish with a squeeze of lemon juice and garnish with baby herbs.

Spanner crab meat with sweet corn veloute & pickled zucchini ribbons

Serves: 4
Time: 1½ hours

2 large spanner crabs, about 2 kg (4 lb 8 oz)
or 500 g (1 lb 2 oz) spanner crab meat
8 corn cobs, fresh or frozen
600 ml (21 fl oz) cream
100 g (3 ½ oz) butter
50 ml (1 ¾ fl oz) white vinegar
60 g (2 ¼ oz) sugar
2 small zucchini (courgettes)
zest and juice of 1 lime
3 teaspoons aïoli
3 teaspoons sour cream
2 teaspoons dill powder
salt and pepper, to season

If using whole crabs, cook in boiling water for 8–10 minutes, then refresh in a bowl of cold water. When cool, remove the meat from the shell and legs, taking care not to leave any shards of shell in the meat.

Remove the husks from the corn and cut the kernels off the cob. Place in water to boil for 45 minutes. Drain the corn, then return to the pot with 500 ml (17 fl oz/2 cups) of the cream. Cook until very soft. Place the corn in a blender and blend until very smooth. Strain through a medium fine sieve. Add the butter and blend again to ensure a smooth mixture.

Bring the vinegar, sugar and 100 ml (3 ½ fl oz) of water to the boil. Cook until the sugar is dissolved, then set aside to cool.

Trim the top and bottom of the zucchini and peel into ribbons with a vegetable peeler. Place the ribbons in the cooled pickling liquid.

Warm the crab meat with the remaining 100 ml (3 ½ fl oz) cream and the lime juice and pepper. Cool, then add the aïoli and sour cream.

To serve, place the sauce on individual serving plates. Use a serving ring to make a neat circle of crab on each plate. Top the crab with rolls of the pickled zucchini, sprinkle with dill powder and lime zest to garnish.

Spiced grilled octopus with black garlic purée & pickled cucumber

Serves: 4
Time: 2 ½ hours

1 onion, sliced

6 garlic cloves

6 bay leaves

½ teaspoon cumin seeds

½ teaspoon coriander seeds

peel of 1 lemon

1 kg (2 lb 4 oz) octopus

1 litre (35 fl oz/4 cups) olive oil

10 black garlic cloves

200 g (7 oz) sour cream

juice of 1 lemon

salt and pepper, to season

edible flowers, to garnish

Pickled cucumber

1 telegraph (long) cucumber, peeled and shaved

1 teaspoon sugar syrup

4 teaspoon white vinegar

Place the onion, garlic, bay leaves, cumin, coriander and lemon peel in bottom of a large pot. Place the octopus on top and cover with the olive oil. Cook over low heat for 1–2 hours, or until octopus is tender. When octopus is tender, remove and set aside to cool. The liquid can be reused again.

Blend the black garlic with the sour cream, then add the lemon juice and salt and pepper to taste. Transfer to a squeeze bottle for serving.

To make the pickled cucumber, combine the cucumber, sugar syrup and vinegar just before serving.

To serve, portion the octopus tentacles and place in the center of a plate. Squeeze the black garlic on one side and place the cucumber pickles on the other side. Garnish with edible flowers.

Oysters with burnt eggplant
& lemon fluid gel

Serves: 4
Time: 1 hour, plus overnight cooling

24 oysters
baby herbs, to garnish

Burnt eggplant

1 large eggplant (aubergine)
2 garlic cloves
1 lemon, juice
½ teaspoon cumin
½ teaspoon sea salt
1 teaspoon plain yoghurt

Lemon fluid gel

200 ml (7 fl oz) lemon juice
100 g (3 ½ oz) sugar
1 teaspoon agar agar powder
50 ml (1 ¾ fl oz) lemon juice
10 g (¼ oz) sugar
2 g (1/8 oz) xanthan gum

———————

Shuck the oysters or get your fishmonger to do this. Rinse in ice water and store in the fridge.

Burn the eggplant over a gas flame or on the barbecue until the skin is thoroughly charred and the flesh is soft and tender,. This should take about 4 minutes per side, depending on the size of the eggplant. Set aside in a bowl to cool.

When the eggplant has cooled, peel the blackened skin and discard. Place the flesh of the eggplant in a blender with the garlic, lemon juice to taste, cumin, sea salt and yoghurt. Blend until smooth and set aside for serving.

in a blender. Heat the 50 ml (1 ¾ fl oz) lemon juice and 10 g (¼ oz) sugar until the sugar is dissolved. Mix the xanthan gum into the hot liquid, then add to the blender with the cooled gel. Blend until a smooth gel consistency is achieved. Pour into a squeeze bottle for serving.

To serve, place some ice on a plate and place the oysters in their shells on top. Squeeze the burnt eggplant on one half of each oyster and lemon fluid gel on the other half. Sprinkle with baby herbs to garnish.

Whitebait with mountain salad & crushed pistachio

Serves: 6–8
Time: 30 minutes

1 kg (2 lb 4 oz) whitebait, washed and drained
500 g (1 lb 2 oz) cornflour (cornstarch)
100 g (3 ½ oz) rice flour
1 teaspoon cayenne pepper
1 teaspoon ground coriander
1 teaspoon ground cumin
4 teaspoon celery salt
1 litre (35 fl oz/4 cups) oil, for frying
1 iceberg lettuce, cut into quarters
3 tablespoons pistachio powder
lime cheeks, to serve
chopped dill and watermelon radish, to garnish

Dressing
2 garlic cloves, crushed
juice of 1 lemon
100 g (3½ oz) plain yoghurt
salt and pepper, to season
3 saffron threads

Combine the flours with the spices and mix well. Dredge the whitebait in the seasoned flour, then remove the excess by shaking in the strainer.

Fry the whitebait in the oil until golden and crisp. Drain on paper towel.

To make the dressing, mix the garlic and lemon juice into the yoghurt. Season with salt and pepper.

To serve, place a quarter lettuce on each plate and drizzle with the yoghurt dressing. Dust with the pistachio powder and garnish with dill. Add the whitebait to the plate and serve with lime cheeks on the side.

(Mountain salad pictured on p98.)

Fresh fig, Serrano Parma ham & goat cheese with balsamic emulsion

Serves: 4
Time: 20 minutes

16 slices Serrano Parma ham
4 black figs, peeled and cut into quarters
200 g (7 oz) goat ash cheese
1 watermelon radish, thinly sliced
1 tablespoon micro basil
edible flowers, to garnish

Balsamic emulsion
50 ml (1 ¾ fl oz) balsamic vinegar
50 g (1 ¾ oz) brown sugar
50 ml (1 ¾ fl oz) oil
50 ml (1 ¾ fl oz) lemon juice

Add all of the balsamic emulsion ingredients to a blender and mix until combined and the sugar is dissolved.

To serve, arrange the ham in a circle on each plate. Top with the quarters of fig and crumbled goat cheese. Drizzle with the balsamic emulsion and garnish with radish slices, micro basil.

Vegetable Nayeh

(V)
Serves: 4–6
Time: 4–5 hours

100 g (3½ oz) onion pickle
1 punnet heirloom tomatoes (green, red and yellow), sliced
1 finger lime (sliced in half, with the pulp squeezed out)
30 candied walnuts baby herbs and edible flowers, to garnish (optional), (see note)

Rice crackers
180 g (6½ oz/1 cup) jasmine rice
1 teaspoon Tabasco sauce
½ teaspoon citric acid
½ teaspoon salt

Avocado purée
3 avocados
juice of 2 lemons
1 teaspoon sugar
pinch of salt

Cook the jasmine rice with 500 ml (17 fl oz/2 cups) of water in a heavy-based pan over high heat for 5–10 minutes, stirring constantly. Reduce the heat and add a further 750 ml (26 fl oz/3 cups) of water bit by bit. Cook for a further 30–40 minutes, or until soft. Remove from the heat.

Preheat the oven to 100°C (200°F). Lightly grease a baking tray and line with baking paper. Add the Tabasco sauce, citric acid and salt to the rice. Place in a blender and blend until very smooth. Spread a thin layer of the mixture on the tray. Cook for 2.5–3 hours, depending on your oven. Remove from the oven and allow to cool. Break into large pieces and shallow-fry over very high heat until puffed.

To make the avocado purée, peel the avocado and scoop out the flesh. Add the avocado, lemon juice, sugar and salt to a blender and purée until smooth. Pour into a squeeze bottle.

To assemble, place a drop of avocado purée on the plate and top with a rice cracker. Place the pickled onion and heirloom tomatoes on top, then squeeze the avocado purée on top.

Sprinkle with finger limes and garnish with baby herbs, candied walnuts and edible flowers (optional).

the rice. Place in a blender and blend until very smooth. Spread a thin layer of the mixture on the tray. Cook for 2.5–3 hours, depending on your oven. Remove from the oven and allow to cool. Break into large pieces and shallow-fry over very high heat until puffed.

To make the avocado purée, peel the avocado and scoop out the flesh. Add the avocado, lemon juice, sugar and salt to a blender and purée until smooth. Pour into a squeeze bottle.

To assemble, place a drop of avocado purée on the plate and top with a rice cracker. Place the pickled onion and heirloom tomatoes on top, then squeeze the avocado purée on top.

Sprinkle with finger limes and garnish with baby herbs, candied walnuts and edible flowers (optional).

Onion pickle

125 g (4½ oz/½ cup) sugar
1 large Spanish (red) onion, sliced
125 ml (4 fl oz/½ cup) white vinegar

To make the onion pickle, add the sugar and 250 ml (9 fl oz/1 cup) of water to a saucepan and heat until the sugar is dissolved. Add the sliced onions and vinegar, then set aside.

**Note: Make at least one day in advance.
This can be stored in the fridge in an airtight container for up to 4 weeks.**

Arabic lentil soup
with coriander & yoghurt

Serves: 6–8
Time: 45 minutes

200 g (7 oz) red lentils
1 teaspoon ground turmeric
1 teaspoon ground coriander
6 garlic cloves, crushed
1 large brown onion
50 g (1 ¾ oz) oil
6 tomatoes, chopped
1 bunch coriander (cilantro), chopped
50 g (1 ¾ oz) ghee
1 teaspoon cumin seed
250 g (9 oz/1 cup) plain yoghurt
salt and pepper, to season

Rinse the lentils well until the water runs clear. Cook the lentils in 1.5 litres (52 fl oz/6 cups) of water with the turmeric and coriander for about 30 minutes over medium heat, or until they start to break down. Set aside until needed.

In a separate pan, sauté 4 garlic cloves and the onion in oil. Add the chopped tomatoes and half the coriander, then mix with the lentils. Season to taste.

Heat the ghee in a frying pan over medium heat and add the remaining 2 garlic cloves and the cumin seeds. Cook until fragrant, taking care not to burn the garlic. Add to the lentil mix.

To serve, place the lentil soup into bowls and top with a dollop of yoghurt and the remaining coriander to garnish.

45

Zucchini flowers stuffed with king prawns in a bouillabaisse emulsion

Serves: 4
Time: 1 hour

400 g (14 oz) prawn (shrimp) meat
100 g (3 ½ oz) white fish
1 garlic clove, crushed
2 teaspoons grated ginger
50 ml (1 ¾ fl oz) cream
zest and juice of 1 lemon
50 g (1 ¾ oz) butter, softened
12 zucchini (courgette) flowers
1.5 litres (52 fl oz/6 cups) oil, for frying
100 g (3 ½ oz) baby herbs, to garnish

Batter
200 g (6 ⅔ oz) self-raising (self-rising) flour
300 ml (10½ fl oz) soda water

Bouillabaisse emulsion
200 g (7 oz) butter
1 large onion, chopped
4 garlic cloves, crushed
1 carrot, diced
1 celery stick, diced
500 g (1 lb 2 oz) tinned diced tomatoes
200 g (7 oz) mussels
500 g (1 lb 2 oz) fish heads
100 g (3 ½ oz) prawn (shrimp) heads
a few threads saffron
1 teaspoon chopped chives
salt and pepper, to season

Blend the prawn meat and white fish in a blender, then add the garlic, ginger, cream, lemon zest, half the lemon juice and the butter. Mix well and season to taste. Place the prawn mixture in a piping bag.

Trim the ends of the zucchini flowers and remove the stamen from inside the flower. Pipe approximately 50 g (1 ¾ oz) of prawn mixture into each flower. Set aside.

To make the bouillabaisse emulsion, heat 50 g (1 ¾ oz) of the butter in a pan over medium heat. Add the onion, garlic, carrot and celery and sauté until softened. Add the tinned tomatoes, mussels, fish heads and prawn heads and 1 litre (35 fl oz/4 cups) of water. Simmer for 25 minutes, then strain the liquid into a pan. Place the pan over medium heat and cook until reduced by half. Allow to cool slightly before blending the stock. Add the saffron and remaining 150 g (5½ oz) butter and season to taste. Set aside.

Dip the flower end of the zucchini in the batter and drain off any excess. Heat the oil in a deep frying pan to 180°C (350°F). Deep fry for 2–3 minutes on each side, then drain off any excess oil on paper towel.

To serve, pour the broth into individual bowls and top with the zucchini flowers. Garnish with the baby herbs.

Note: Mussels can be salty so don't add any salt until the bouillabaisse is finished, otherwise it may become oversalted.

CHAPTER 2

Main Course

Forbidden black rice with porcini fluid gel

Serves: 4 (Entrée serves: 8)
Time: 1 hour

200 g (7 oz/1 cup) black wild rice
200 g (7 oz) mixed mushrooms, sliced
100 g (3 ½ oz) butter
1 garlic clove, crushed
1 diced shallot
100 ml (7 fl oz) cream
juice of 1 lemon
½ teaspoon porcini powder
micro herbs, to garnish
salt and pepper, to season

Porcini fluid gel
100 ml (3 ½ fl oz) cream
½ teaspoon porcini powder
2 g (1/8 oz) xanthan gum

Add the rice and 500 ml (17 fl oz/2 cups) of water to a heavy-based saucepan set over medium heat. Cook the rice for about 30 minutes, or until tender. Spread the rice over a baking tray to cool.

To make the porcini fluid gel, place the cream and porcini powder in a saucepan and bring to the boil. Add the xanthum gum and remove from the heat. Allow to cool slightly, then put in a blender and blend until smooth. Transfer to a squeeze bottle.

Heat the butter in a frying pan over medium heat. Add the mushrooms and sauté. Add the garlic and shallot, then add 100 ml (3 ½ fl oz) cream, ½ teaspoon porcini powder, and season with salt and pepper. Add the rice and sauté for a few minutes.

To serve, divide the rice into four portions, top with the porcini fluid gel and a squeeze of lemon juice. Garnish with micro herbs.

Confit Muscovy duck Maryland

Serves: 4
Time: 3 hours, plus 6 hours curing time

1 kg (2 lb 4 oz) Muscovy duck Maryland
(4 pieces)
100 g (3 ½ oz) sea salt
1 white onion, peeled
2 cinnamon quills
2 bay leaves
250 ml (9 fl oz/1 cup) white wine
8 Dutch orange carrots, peeled
8 Dutch yellow carrots, peeled
4 figs, sliced into quarters
50 g (1 ¾ oz) butter
Edible flowers, to garnish

Sauce

1 litre (35 fl oz/4 cups) orange juice
50 g (1 ¾ oz) sugar
100 ml (3 ½ fl oz) Grand Marnier
1 orange, zested

Dry the duck with paper towel, rub well with sea salt and place on a rack. Cover and leave for 6 hours to cure.

Preheat the oven to 180°C (350°F). Remove the salt from the duck and place in a roasting pan with the onion, cinnamon, bay leaves and white wine. Cover with baking paper, then seal the pan well with foil. Roast for 2 hours.

To make the sauce, boil the orange juice until reduced by half. Add the sugar and keep reducing until a syrupy texture. Add the Grand Marnier and orange zest. Remove from the heat and set aside until needed.

Blanch the carrots and coat with the butter.

To serve, place the duck in center of a plate and add 2 of each carrot and a few fig quarters. Drizzle the sauce on top of the duck Maryland. Garnish with edible flowers.

Djel Mishwe with cracked wheat salad & lemon mustard vinaigrette
(chargrilled corn-fed chicken breast)

Serves: 4
Time: 1 hour, plus marinade time

4 pieces corn-fed chicken breast
10 garlic cloves, crushed
zest and juice of 1 lemon
20 ml (¾ fl oz) olive oil
60 ml (2 fl oz) white vinegar
1 teaspoon salt
pepper, to season

Salad
200 g (7 oz) cracked wheat (burghul)
1 red tomato, de-seeded and diced
1 yellow tomato, de-seeded and diced
4 teaspoons chopped chives
4 teaspoons chopped flat-leaf (Italian) parsley
4 teaspoons sumac

Dressing
45 ml (1 ½ fl oz) dijon mustard
120 ml (4 fl oz) lemon juice
½ teaspoon sugar
a few drops of Tabasco sauce
30 ml (1 fl oz) extra virgin olive oil
salt and pepper, to season

Place the chicken, garlic, lemon, olive oil, white vinegar and salt and pepper in a large bowl and mix to coat chicken. Leave to marinate at least 4–5 hours.

To make the dressing, combine all of the ingredients and set aside until needed.

Preheat the oven to 180°C (350°F). Pat the chicken dry with paper towel before char-grilling at high heat on barbecue or grill pan. Cook for 3 minutes on each side, then transfer to the oven for 10–12 minutes, depending on the thickness of the chicken.

To make the salad, soak the burghul in 500 ml (17 fl oz/2 cups) of water for 30 minutes. Bring 500 ml (17 fl oz/2 cups) of water to the boil, then remove from the heat. Strain the burghul, then blanch in the boiled water for 3–4 minutes. Strain and set aside to cool. Combine the tomato, chives, parsley and sumac with the burghul. Add half of the dressing and mix well to combine.

To serve, place the salad in a sharing bowl and place the chicken on a shared serving platter. Serve the remaining dressing in a bowl on the side.

Samke harra barramundi with saffron potatoes

Serves: 4
Time: 45 minutes

4 pieces barramundi, skin on, boneless (about 200 g/7 oz each)
600 g (1 lb 5 oz) kipfler (fingerling) potatoes, peeled
a few threads of saffron
100 ml (3 ½ fl oz) olive oil
micro coriander (cilantro), to garnish
avocado fluid gel, to garnish
(optional, see page 12)

Harra (hot sauce)
1 bunch flat-leaf (Italian) parsley, finely chopped
1 bunch coriander (cilantro), finely chopped
1 bunch garlic chives, finely chopped
3 long red chilies, finely chopped
6 garlic cloves, finely chopped
100 g (3 ½ oz) barberries
juice and zest of 1 lime
salt and pepper, to season

To make the harra, sauté the parsley, coriander, garlic chives, chilies and garlic in a pan with 60 ml (2 fl oz) oil over low heat until soft. Add the barberries, lemon juice and zest. Purée in blender until smooth, then add salt and pepper to taste.

Boil the potatoes with the saffron for 8–10 minutes, or until tender, depending on the size of the potatoes. Strain and dice to your preferred size. Dress with 1 tablespoon of oil and salt and pepper to taste.

Preheat the oven to 180°C (350°F). Place 1 tablespoon of oil in a non-stick frying pan and dust with sea salt. Place the barramundi skin side down and cook for 3 minutes. Place in the oven for a further 4 minutes, then turn the fish over and rest for a few minutes.

To serve, place the warm potatoes in the middle of the plate, top with the fish placed skin side up and squeeze the harra dressing over the fish. Garnish with micro coriander and avocado fluid gel (optional).

Organic bamboo rice
with heirloom green vegetables
& black garlic fluid gel

Serves: 4
Time: 45 minutes

3 garlic cloves, crushed
1 white onion, finely diced
4 teaspoon ghee
200 g (7 oz) bamboo rice
500 ml (17 fl oz/2 cups) vegetable stock
1 bunch broccolini
1 bunch green asparagus
2 zucchini (courgettes)
50 g (1 ¾ oz) butter
salt and pepper, to season
micro coriander (cilantro), to garnish

Black garlic fluid gel
8 black garlic cloves
100 ml (3 ½ fl oz) double cream
2 g (1/8 oz) xanthan gum
salt and pepper, to season

Sauté the garlic and onion in a pan with the ghee until translucent. Add the rice and cook for a few minutes. Add the vegetable stock, one ladle at a time, until rice is just cooked. Set aside until needed.

Peel the bottom stem of the broccolini and asparagus. Scoop out balls from the zucchini using a melon baller. Blanch all of the vegetables in boiling water, then drain. Melt the butter in a pan and add the vegetables, tossing gently to coat. Season with salt and pepper.

To make the black garlic fluid gel, heat the garlic and cream in a saucepan and bring to the boil. Season with salt and pepper.
Add the xanthan gum and blend with a hand blender. Pour the mixture in a squeeze bottle for serving.

To serve, place a serving ring in the center of the plate and add rice to make a circular platform. Arrange the vegetables on top of the rice and squeeze the black garlic gel on top. Garnish with micro coriander.

Wagyu corned beef

Serves: 4
Time: 4 hours

1 kg (2 lb 4 oz) Wagyu corned beef
3 tablespoons tomato paste (concentrated purée)
3 tablespoons brown sugar
2 cinnamon sticks
2 bay leaves
6–8 juniper berries
500 ml (17 fl oz/2 cups) balsamic vinegar
1 teaspoon chopped flat-leaf (Italian) parsley

Sauce

4 shallots, peeled and finely diced
50 g (1 ¾ oz) butter
drizzle of olive oil
3 tablespoons seeded mustard
500 ml (17 fl oz/2 cups) double cream
pinch of white pepper

Vegetables

1 bunch Dutch mixed carrots (baby)
1 bunch baby turnips
8 Brussels sprouts
50 g (1 ¾ oz) butter
salt and pepper, to season

Add the tomato paste, brown sugar, cinnamon, bay leaves, juniper berries, balsamic vinegar and 2–3 litres (70–102 fl oz/8–12 cups) of water to a heavy-based saucepan set over high heat. Bring to the boil, then reduce the heat to low and add the beef. Cook for 2–3 hours, then remove the meat from the liquid and set aside to rest.

To make the sauce, sauté the shallots in butter and oil for a few minutes. Add the mustard and stir for another few minutes, then add the cream and season with pepper. Keep stirring constantly until reduced by half, then set aside.

To make the vegetables, peel and dice all the vegetables. Blanch until cooked to your taste, crunchy or softer. Add butter and salt to taste.

To serve, slice the corned beef into four portions and plate. Add the vegetables, sauce and garnish with chopped parsley.

Soft shell crab with chili tomato jam

Serves: 4
Time: 45 minutes, plus chili jam: 1 hour

8 soft shell crabs, cleaned and gutted
100 g (3 ½ oz) cornflour (cornstarch)
1 litre (35 fl oz/4 cups) oil, for frying
salt and pepper, to season

Batter
300 ml (10 ½ fl oz) soda water (club soda)
120 g (4 oz) self-raising (self-rising) flour

Vegetable ribbon salad
1 telegraph (long) cucumber
1 daikon radish
1 yellow carrot
1 purple carrot

Chili tomato jam
300 ml (10 ½ fl oz) red wine
200 g (7 oz) brown sugar
2 bird's eye chilies, chopped
500 ml (17 fl oz/2 cups) lemon juice
3 cinnamon sticks
800 g (1 lb 12 oz) tinned peeled tomatoes, drained

To make the chili tomato jam, add the wine, brown sugar, chilies, lemon juice and cinnamon to a saucepan Bring to the boil and cook until reduced by half. Reduce the heat, add the tomatoes and continue to cook until further reduced and a jammy consistency is reached. Allow to cool.

To make the vegetable ribbon salad, peel the vegetables into long ribbons using a peeler or mandolin. Soak in ice-water until required.

To make the batter, whisk the flour and soda water together until smooth.

Dust the cleaned and dried crab with cornflour and salt and pepper. Dip each crab in the batter and place into the deep fryer separately (do not overcrowd the pan). Cook at 180°C (350°F) until golden, then drain on paper towel.

To serve, place the crab on top of the ribbon salad. Add the chili jam in a small ramekin on the side.

Farro, walnut, gorgonzola & cavolo nero

Serves: 4
Time: 30 minutes

1 bunch cavolo nero
50 g (1 ¾ oz) snow peas
50 g (1 ¾ oz) sugar snap peas
200 g (7 oz) farro
50 ml (1 ¾ fl oz) double cream
100 g (3 ½ oz) gorgonzola
50 g (1 ¾ oz) butter
1 garlic clove, crushed
zest and juice of 1 lemon
1 handful walnuts
salt and pepper, to season

Boil 1 litre (35 fl oz/4 cups) of water in a saucepan over medium heat. Blanch the cavolo nero, snow peas and sugar snap peas for 1 minute. Reserve the water. Remove the vegetables and refresh in ice-water. Drain and set aside until needed.

Remove the stems from the cavolo nero and chop into bite size pieces.

Using the reserved boiled water, boil the farro for 10–12 minutes, or until cooked al dente. Drain and set aside.

Warm the cream and gorgonzola, then add the farro and season to taste.

Melt the butter in a pan with the garlic and lemon zest. Toss the vegetables through until coated and add a squeeze of lemon juice.

To serve, place the farro in a serving bowl, top with the vegetables and sprinkle the walnuts over the top.

Slow-braised lamb neck with slow-cooked eggplant

Serves: 4
Time: 5 hours

2 lamb necks (around 2kg/4 lb 8 oz)
50 g (1 ¾ oz) cornflour (cornstarch)
50 ml (1 ¾ fl oz) oil
1 large onion, peeled and diced
1 large carrot, peeled and diced
1 celery stick, diced
6 garlic cloves, crushed
4 bay leaves
500 g (1 lb 2 oz) tinned diced tomatoes
1 litre (35 fl oz/4 cups) red wine
100 g (3 ½ oz) ghee
4 garlic cloves
2 large eggplants (aubergines), peeled and diced
1 long red chili, chopped
1 bunch flat-leaf (Italian) parsley, chopped
2 watermelon radishes, sliced
2 red radishes, sliced
salt and pepper, to season
micro parsley, to garnish

Note: This dish can be served with rice, mashed potato or bread.

Dust the lamb necks with cornflour. Add half the oil to a pan and sear the lamb until browned all over, then set aside. Add the remaining oil to the same pan and sauté the onion, carrot and celery and garlic over low heat until softened.

Preheat the oven to 150°C (300°F). Add the bay leaves, tomatoes and wine to the pan and bring to the boil. Remove from the heat and add the lamb. Cover with foil and cook in the oven for 3–4 hours.

Remove the meat, strain the sauce and reserve for another use. Retain the vegetables for the eggplant but remove the bay leaves. Remove the meat from the bones and set aside for serving.

Melt the ghee in a saucepan and add the garlic, then the eggplant and chili. Cover and cook over low heat until tender. Add the reserved vegetables that were cooked with the meat and stir through. Season to taste and add the chopped parsley.

To serve, spread a layer of eggplant in a serving dish. Top with half the shredded lamb, then the remaining eggplant and a final layer of the remaining lamb. Garnish with sliced radish and micro parsley.

Souvlaki-style lamb backstrap served with eggplant chips, chickpea purée & rocket salad

Serves: 4
Time: 40 minutes, plus marinating time

2 garlic cloves, crushed

zest and juice of 1 lemon

1 teaspoon finely chopped oregano

4 tablespoons extra virgin olive oil

800 g (1 lb 12 oz) lamb backstrap, denuded

1 large eggplant (aubergine)

100 g (3 ½ oz) cornflour (cornstarch)

500 ml (17 fl oz/2 cups) vegetable oil, for frying

400 g (14 oz) tinned chickpeas, drained

1 garlic clove

200 g (7 oz) wild baby rocket (arugula)

1 shallot, sliced

100 g (3 ½ oz) feta cheese

salt and pepper, to season

Combine the garlic, lemon zest, oregano and 1 tablespoon of the oil. Add the lamb and marinade for at least 2 hours, or overnight.

Peel the eggplant and slice finely with a mandolin. Blot any excess moisture with paper towel. Dust the slices in cornflour. Fry the eggplant in vegetable oil until crisp and golden.

Add the chickpeas and garlic to a blender with half the lemon juice. Purée until smooth.

Combine the rocket, sliced shallot and crumbled feta in a bowl.

Mix the remaining lemon juice with remaining 3 tablespoons of oil. Add to the salad just before serving.

Chargrill the lamb over high heat for 2–3 minutes, depending on the thickness. Turn over and cook a further 2 minutes, or until cooked to your liking. Rest for 5 minutes.

To serve, slice the lamb and place 200 g (7 oz) per plate. Add a quenelle of chickpea purée to the side, with a portion of the dressed salad. Add eggplant chips to the plate.

Chargrilled swordfish with kipfler potato, artichokes, kale & cherry tomatoes

Serves: 4
Time: 1 hour

500 g (17 ½ oz) kipfler (fingerling) potatoes, peeled
400 g (14 oz) tinned artichokes, drained and cut into quarters
250 g (9 oz) cherry tomatoes
1 large handful kale, chopped (optional)
200 ml (7 fl oz) fish stock
200 ml (7 fl oz) white wine
100 g (3 ½ oz) unsalted butter
salt and pepper, to season
4 pieces swordfish, 200 g (7 oz) each
canola oil spray

Boil 500 ml (17 fl oz/2 cups) of water in a saucepan over medium heat. Add the kale and blanch for 1 minute, or until tender. Reserve the water for the tomatoes. Remove the kale from the pan and cool in ice water, then drain.

Cut a small cross on the bottom of each cherry tomato. Blanch in the same water for 10–15 seconds, then refresh in ice-water. Remove the skin and set aside.

Add the potatoes to the same water and cook until tender. Refresh in ice water, then drain and set aside. Crush the potatoes and mix together with the swordfish.

Spray fish with the oil spray. Chargrill the fish on a hot barbecue grill or in a chargrill pan until both sides are grill marked. Set aside.

Heat the fish stock and white wine in a saucepan over medium heat. Cook until reduced by three-quarters. Add the butter. Place the swordfish in the stock for 1 minute to finish cooking, then remove and set aside. Add the vegetables to the stock until warmed through, then remove.

To serve, place the vegetables on the plate, add the fish on top and some of the reduced stock over the top.

Tunisian pastry-wrapped free range duck Maryland
with Grand Marnier sauce

Serves: 4
Time: 1 hour

2 duck Marylands (see confit Muscovy duck
Maryland, p54)
1 white onion, sliced
2 garlic cloves, crushed
50 g (1 ¾ oz) butter
1 handful raisins
1 tablespoon diced dried apricot
1 tablespoon finely chopped flat-leaf (Italian)
parsley
1 tablespoon honey
4 sheets brick pastry
salt and pepper, to season
1 tablespoon almond flakes, to garnish
1 tablespoon micro herbs, to garnish

Sauce
200 ml (7 fl oz) orange juice
2 tablespoons orange marmalade
50 ml (1 ¾ fl oz) Grand Marnier

Remove the duck meat from the bone and
shred.

Preheat the oven to 180°C (350°F). Line a
baking tray with baking paper.

Sauté the onions and garlic in butter until soft
and golden. Add the shredded duck meat. Mix
well, then add the raisins, apricots, parsley and
honey. Drain any excess liquid. Place the duck
mixture along the pastry and roll into a cigar
shape. Repeat with the remaining mixture and
pastry.

Place the pastry rolls on the baking tray and
bake for 4–5 minutes, or until crisp.

To make the sauce, heat the orange juice in a
saucepan over medium heat and reduce down
until a quarter of the original volume. Add in
the marmalade and Grand Mariner and set
aside.

To serve, place the pastry rolls on plates and
drizzle with Grand Marnier sauce. Garnish with
the almond flakes and micro herbs.

Organic garlic lemon chicken breast

Serves: 4
Time: 1 hour

1 kg (2 lb 4 oz) organic chicken breasts (4
pieces, 250 g/9 oz each, skin on optional)
4 tablespoons olive oil
zest of 1 lemon
8 garlic cloves, crushed
10 lime leaves
½ teaspoon sea salt
½ teaspoon white pepper
4 tablespoons white vinegar
micro herbs, to garnish
seasonal vegetables, to garnish

Sauce
375 ml (13 fl oz/1 ½ cups) chicken broth
80 g (2 ¾ oz) unsalted butter
2 g (1/8 oz) xanthan gum thickener

Preheat the oven to 180°C (350°F). Marinate
the chicken in the olive oil and seasoning.

Transfer to a baking tray and cook for 15
minutes. Remove the chicken and reserve the
broth for the sauce.

Cook the chicken on a barbecue grill or in a
chargrill pan over high heat until the skin is
crisp.

To make the sauce, place the broth, butter and
xanthan gum in blender to combine.

To serve, place the chicken on a serving platter
with the sauce separately on the side. Garnish
with seasonal vegetables and micro herbs.

Al Kabsa
(traditional Saudi Arabian rice & meat dish)

Serves: 4
Time: 4 hours

1.6 kg (3 lb 8 oz) beef cheeks
100 g (3 ½ oz) butter
1 onion, chopped
8 garlic cloves, crushed
2 star anise
2 cinnamon sticks
1 teaspoon ground cumin
1 teaspoon ground coriander
4 tablespoons tomato paste
(concentrated purée)
2 bay leaves
2 long red chilies, chopped
2 black dried lemons
50 ml (1 ¾ fl oz) vinegar
200 g (7 oz) basmati rice
salt and pepper, to season
1 handful roasted almonds, to garnish
2 onions, for frying, to garnish
1 handful mint and coriander (cilantro)
leaves, to garnish
250 g (9 oz/1 cup) Greek-style yoghurt,
to serve

Sear the beef cheeks in a heavy based pan over medium heat.

In a separate pan, melt the butter over medium heat and sauté the onions and garlic.

Add the spices, tomato paste, bay leaves, chilies, dried lemons and vinegar. Sauté gently for a few minutes.

Add the beef, then 2 litres (70 fl oz/8 cups) water. Cook, covered, over high heat for 20 minutes. Cook for a further 2½ hours, or until the meat is tender. Add salt and pepper to taste. Remove the meat and strain the stock, reserving the stock for the rice.

Wash the rice and place in saucepan with the beef stock. Bring to the boil over high heat, then cover and cook over low heat for 8–12 minutes.

Place the rice on a large serving plate, place beef cheeks on top of the rice. Sprinkle roasted almonds, fried onion and mint on beef cheeks. Finish the dish with Greek-style yoghurt on the side.

78

Sheikel Mish, braised deboned short rib with Red Foo potato & grilled asparagus

Serves: 4
Time: 4 hour

1.2 kg (2 lb 12 oz) Black Angus short ribs
1 onion
1 carrot
1 celery stick
1 leek
6 garlic cloves, crushed
1 handful juniper berries
1 teaspoon peppercorns
6 bay leaves
1 teaspoon smoked paprika
1 litre (35 fl oz/4 cups) red wine
500 g (1 lb 2 oz) puréed tomato
8 Red Foo potatoes
100 g (3 ½ oz) butter
2 bunches green asparagus
salt and pepper, to season
2 red radishes, to garnish
micro herbs, to garnish

Preheat the oven to 160°C (315°F).

Sear the short ribs in a heavy-based pan over medium heat. Transfer to a large deep baking tray.

Sauté the onion, carrot, celery, leek and spices in the same pan, then add to the meat. Pour the red wine, tomato paste and 1 litre (35 fl oz/4 cups) of water in the tray to almost cover the meat. Seal the tray with baking paper and foil and cook for 3–4 hours.

Remove the tray from the oven and remove the bones from the meat while still warm. Strain the sauce, add to a saucepan and reduce until the desired sauce consistency is reached.

Boil the potatoes for 10–12 minutes, or until tender. Drain the potatoes and remove the skin. Sauté with 50 g (1 ¾ oz) of the butter in a pan over medium heat. Season with salt and pepper, to taste. Trim and peel the ends of the asparagus. Blanch in boiling water for 1 minute, then drain. Sauté with remaining 50 g (1 ¾ oz) of the butter in a pan over medium heat. Season with salt and pepper, to taste. Finely slice the radishes on a mandolin. To serve, place the deboned short rib on the plate. Place the potatoes and asparagus next to the meat and add the sauce over the meat. Garnish with slices of radish and micro herbs.

Slow-cooked lamb shoulder with sautéed broccolini & French puy lentil & tomato salad

Serves: 4
Time: 3 hours and 20 minutes

Lamb

1.6 kg (3 lb 8 oz) bone in lamb shoulder (4 pieces)
2 large onions, peeled and diced
2 carrots
2 celery sticks
6 bay leaves
½ teaspoon cumin
½ teaspoon coriander
½ teaspoon Chinese five-spice
500 ml (17 fl oz/2 cups) red wine
100 g (3 ½ oz) tomato paste (concentrated purée)
100 ml (3 fl oz) oil
salt and pepper, to season
2 bunches broccolini
1 garlic clove
50 g (1 ¾ oz) butter

Lentil & tomato salad

200 g (7 oz) French puy lentils
4 roma (plum) tomatoes, chopped
1 bunch chives, chopped
1 yellow capsicum (pepper), chopped
1 lemon, juice
salt and pepper, to season

Preheat the oven to 160°C (315°F). Sear the lamb in half the oil in a heavy-based pan or casserole dish. Remove the lamb and set aside.

In the same pan, sauté the onion, carrot, celery, bay leaves and spices. Return the lamb to the pan with the red wine and reduce the wine slightly. Add the tomato paste and 1.5 litres (52 fl oz/6 cups) of water. Cover tightly and bake for 2–3 hours.

Remove the meat and strain the remaining sauce. Refrigerate the sauce overnight to remove fat from the top or, if using straight away, skim or drain any fat off the top. Reduce the sauce in a pan until the desired thickness for serving.

To make the salad, boil the lentils in 1 litre (35 fl oz) of water and salt until al dente. Strain. Add the tomatoes, chives and capsicum to the lentils and season with salt and pepper. Add the lemon juice and the remaining oil at the last minute.

Peel the ends of the broccolini and blanch in boiling water for 1 minute. Drain and sauté with the garlic and butter. Season to taste.

To serve, plate the lamb with sauce on a serving platter. Place the broccolini and lentils in separate serving bowls to serve family style.

Spiced sweet pork belly with tomato chili jam & balsamic emulsion

Serves: 4
Time: 3 hours

3 cinnamon quills
4 whole star anise
5 bay leaves
500 ml (17 fl oz/2 cups) white wine
1 whole pork belly, large 2–3kg (4 lb 8 oz–6 lb 12 oz)
salt, to taste
baby herbs, to garnish

Tomato chili jam

500 ml (17 fl oz/2 cups) white wine
1 cinnamon quill
1 star anise
1 bay leaf
200 g (7 oz) sugar
160 ml (5 ¼ fl oz) vinegar
1 kg (2 lb 4 oz) green tomato, chopped
3–4 long red chilies

Balsamic emulsion

500 g (1 lb 2 oz) sugar
500 ml (17 fl oz/2 cups) balsamic vinegar
100 ml (3 ½ fl oz) lemon juice

Preheat the oven to 180°C (350°F).

Place the cinnamon, star anise, bay leaves and wine in the bottom of a roasting pan. Place a rack on top and cover with a layer of baking paper. Place the pork on top, sprinkle with salt and add enough water to come halfway up the pork. Cover with another layer of baking paper and seal with foil over the whole tray. Bake for 2–2½ hours. Remove from the oven, remove the skin and leave to cool.

To make the tomato chili jam, place the wine, cinnamon, star anise, bay leaf, sugar and vinegar in a pan. Bring to the boil and reduce until syrupy. Add the tomatoes and chili. Cook for a few minutes until translucent and set aside.

To make the balsamic emulsion, mix all of the ingredients in a saucepan. Bring to the boil and reduce to a syrup consistency.

Portion the pork into approximately 200 g (7 oz) pieces. Sear the pork in a frying pan on all sides. Drizzle with the balsamic reduction to coat the pork, then transfer to a serving plate. Place a spoonful of tomato chili jam beside the pork and garnish with baby herbs.

Organic chicken tagine
with mograbieh & minted yoghurt

Serves: 4
Time: 45 minutes

1 kg (2 lb 4 oz) organic chicken Maryland
(4 pieces)
100 g (3 ½ oz) ghee
1 onion, finely chopped
2 carrots, finely chopped
1 celery stick, finely chopped
6 garlic cloves, crushed
4 bay leaves
1 cinnamon stick
a few threads saffron
1 teaspoon ground coriander
1 teaspoon ground cumin
½ teaspoon turmeric
½ teaspoon paprika
1 handful dried apricot
½ preserved lemon, finely chopped
1 handful pitted olives
1 bunch coriander (cilantro)
100 g (3 ½ oz) mograbieh
a few saffron threads
50 g (1 ¾ oz) ghee
salt and pepper, to season
micro herbs, to garnish
halved cherry tomatoes, to garnish (optional)

Minted yoghurt

1 bunch mint
100 g (3½ oz) yoghurt
1 garlic clove, chopped

Sear the chicken with the ghee in a heavy-based pan over medium heat, then set aside.

Sauté the onion, carrot, celery and garlic. Then add the bay leaves and spices and 500 ml (17 fl oz/2 cups) of water before adding the chicken back in. Cook in a tagine or covered casserole dish over low heat for about 25 minutes. Add the apricots and cook for a further 10 minutes. When cooked, add the preserved lemon, olives and coriander.

Place the mograbieh, 1 litre (35 fl oz/4 cups) water, salt and saffron in a saucepan. Bring to the boil and cook for 12 minutes. Strain and then sauté with the ghee.

To make the minted yoghurt, pick the leaves from the mint and chop. Add to the blender with the yoghurt and chopped garlic. Add salt to taste and purée until smooth.

To serve, place the mograbieh in a bowl, top with the chicken tagine and vegetables. Add dollops of the minted yoghurt and garnish with micro herbs and halved cherry tomatoes.

Spice braised beef cheeks

Serves: 4
Time: 3 hours

1.6 kg (3 lb 8 oz) Rangers Valley beef cheeks
(400 g/14 oz each)
2 white onions, peeled and diced
1 celery stick, diced
1 carrot, diced
½ leek
2 cinnamon quills
2 star anise
2 dried black lemons
1 litre (35 fl oz/4 cups) beef stock
750 ml (26 fl oz/3 cups) red wine
4 savoy cabbage leaves
4 asparagus tips
50 g (1 ¾ oz) butter
salt and pepper, to season

Cauliflower velouté

1 whole cauliflower
500 ml (17 fl oz/2 cups) cream
150 g (5 ½ oz) butter

Black garlic sauce

1 potato, peeled and boiled
2 tablespoons black garlic paste
100 g (3 ½ oz) butter
2 g (1/8 oz) xanthan gum

———

In a large frying pan over medium heat, sauté the onion, celery, carrot, leek and spices. Transfer to a large saucepan.

Seal the beef cheeks in a frying pan until golden and add to the saucepan with the vegetables. Add the beef stock and wine and slow cook, covered, for 2 ½ hours.

Remove the beef from the pan and set aside until needed. Strain the liquid and return to the pot. Reduce the liquid until it is a sauce consistency, skimming off any fat or impurities from the surface as it reduces.

· ·

To make the cauliflower velouté, cook the cauliflower in 1 litre (35 fl oz/4 cups) of water until tender. Strain and return to the pot. Add the cream and season with salt and pepper. Cook until slightly reduced, then add to a

blender with the butter and purée until smooth.

Blanch the cabbage and asparagus, then add the butter.

. . . .

To make the black garlic sauce, put all ingredients and 100 ml (3 ½ fl oz) boiling water in a blender while the potato is still warm. Purée until smooth and transfer to a squeeze bottle.

To serve, brush the black garlic sauce through the middle of the plate, add the cauliflower velouté to the center and top with the beef and sauce. Place the asparagus on the side and cover the beef with savoy cabbage leaf.

CHAPTER 3

Sides

Fattoush salad
(medley of Arabic vegetables salad)

Serves: 6–8
Time: 30 minutes

250 g (9 oz) yellow heirloom cherry
tomatoes
3 Lebanese (short) cucumbers, diced
1 yellow capsicum (pepper)
1 red capsicum (pepper)
1 green capsicum (pepper)
1 Spanish (red) onion
1 bunch red radish
1 large handful mint leaves
1 large handful purslane
1 cup chopped flat-leaf (Italian) parsley
2 cups chopped Lebanese (flat) bread

Dressing
juice of 1 lemon
2 tablespoons sumac
100 ml (3 ½ fl oz) extra virgin olive oil
1 teaspoon salt
2 garlic cloves, crushed

Cut all vegetables into same sized (bite size)
pieces. Mix in a bowl with the chopped herbs.

To make the dressing, whisk all of the
ingredients together until combined.

Spray the Lebanese bread with canola oil and
cook in 180°C (350°F) oven for 5–10 minutes,
or until crispy.

To serve, mix the dressing through the salad
and place in a serving bowl. Top with the crispy
Lebanese bread.

Pumpkin, haloumi & rocket salad

Serves: 4–6
Time: 30 minutes

1 small Japanese pumpkin, about 500 g
(1 lb 2 oz)
100 ml (3 ½ fl oz) olive oil
500 g (1 lb 2 oz) haloumi cheese, sliced
500 g (1 lb 2 oz) rocket (arugula)
50 ml (1 ¾ fl oz) aged balsamic vinegar
100 g (3 ½ oz) toasted pine nuts
salt and pepper, to season

Preheat the oven to 180°C (350°F).

Cut the pumpkin into small wedges and place
on a baking tray. Coat in olive oil and season
with salt and pepper. Roast for 10–12 minutes,
or until golden and tender.

Sear the haloumi on a griddle pan, then set
aside.

To serve, layer the roast pumpkin, rocket and
haloumi on a serving platter. Repeat layers
until all of the ingredients are used. Drizzle
with olive oil and balsamic vinegar. Sprinkle the
toasted pine nuts over the top to garnish.

Arabic mountain salad

Serves: 6–8
Time: 1½ hours

2 iceberg lettuce
1 telegraph (long) cucumber
1 cup sliced red radish
2 garlic cloves, crushed
4 tablespoons plain yoghurt
4 tablespoons sour cream
juice and zest of 1 lemon
1 teaspoon sea salt
45 g (1 ½ oz/½ cup) pistachio, toasted
½ cup chopped flat-leaf (Italian) parsley
cracked pepper, to taste

Remove the core from the lettuce and break into pieces. Soak in ice water for 1 hour to become very crisp.

Peel the cucumber and slice into ribbons using a vegetable peeler. Drain the lettuce and dry very well. Combine with the radish and cucumber ribbons.

To make the dressing, combine the garlic, yoghurt, sour cream, lemon juice and salt until mixed well.

Toast the almonds in a dry frying pan until golden and toasted.

To serve, place the combined lettuce, radish and cucumber in a bowl. Drizzle with the dressing and garnish with chopped parsley and pistachio. Top with freshly cracked pepper.

Optional: Serve with chicken, prawns or grilled haloumi.

Bastourma, shankleesh & fig salad

Serves: 4
Time: 30 minutes

100 ml (3 ½ fl oz) sherry vinegar
100 ml (3 ½ fl oz) extra virgin olive oil
200 g (7 oz) sliced bastourma (see note)
200 g (7 oz) shankleesh, crumbled (see note)
6 figs, cut into quarters
confetti coriander and target beetroot, to garnish

Combine the vinegar and oil to make a dressing.

To serve, separate the lettuce into individual leaves and divide between four plates. Add the bostourma, crumbed shankleesh and figs in layers.

Drizzle the dressing over the salad, or serve on the side.

Note: Bastourma is a traditionally dry-cured and air-dried prime cut beef topside.

Shankleesh is a type of cow's milk or sheep milk cheese, similar to feta.

Quinoa, spinach, avocado & chicken salad

Serves: 4
Time: 30 minutes

300 g (10 ½ oz) chicken breast fillet
zest and juice of 1 lemon
1 garlic clove
100 g (3 ½ oz) quinoa
100 g (3 ½ oz) baby spinach
50 ml (1 ¾ fl oz) olive oil
1 avocado, finely diced
1 handful flaked almonds (optional)
salt and pepper, to season

Poach the chicken in simmering water with the lemon peel, garlic and a pinch of salt for 10 minutes, or until just cooked through. Remove the chicken, shred and set aside until needed.

Strain the cooking liquid and return to the pan. Add the quinoa and cook for 12 minutes or until puffed. Drain and set aside.

Place the spinach in a bowl with the lemon juice and olive oil. Add the quinoa and mix through.

To serve, place the quinoa on a serving plate. Top with the shredded chicken and diced avocado. Sprinkle flaked almonds over the top to garnish.

Chickpea, parsley & feta salad

Serves: 4–6
Time: 30 minutes, plus soaking over-night

200 g (7 oz) dried chickpeas
¼ teaspoon bicarbonate of soda (baking soda)
1 cup chopped flat-leaf (Italian) parsley
100 ml (3 ½ fl oz) sherry vinegar
200 g (7 oz) feta cheese
50 ml (1 ¾ fl oz) extra virgin olive oil
1 telegraph (long) cucumber, peeled and ribboned
½ teaspoon ground cumin
halved cherry tomatoes, to garnish (optional)

Soak the chickpeas overnight. The next day, drain and add 1.5 litres (52 fl oz/6 cups) water. Bring to the boil and cook for about 15 minutes, or until tender.

Add the bicarbonate of soda, then drain. Combine the chickpeas with all of the remaining ingredients and mix well.

Serve as a salad, vegetarian entrée or as an accompaniment to any main meal.

CHAPTER 4

Dessert

Vacherin meringue

Serves: 6–8
Time: 4 hours

4 egg whites
250 g (9 oz) sugar
1 teaspoon cornflour (cornstarch)
½ teaspoon white vinegar
a few drops of food coloring (optional)

Rhubarb
1 bunch rhubarb
200 g (7 oz) sugar

Mascarpone
500 g (1 lb 2 oz) mascarpone
100 ml (3 ½ fl oz) cream
50 g (1 ¾ oz) sugar

Preheat the oven to 90°C (194°F). Lightly grease a baking tray and line with baking paper.

Whisk the egg whites and sugar together until stiff. Add the cornflour and vinegar and coloring, if desired.

Spread the mixture thinly onto the baking paper lined tray. Bake for 3–4 hours, then cool slightly. Break into pieces. Store in an airtight container at room temperature.

To make the rhubarb, clean the rhubarb and chop into 1 cm (½ in) pieces. Add to a saucepan with the sugar and cook until soft. Set aside to cool.

To make the mascarpone, whisk all of the ingredients together until combined and the sugar is dissolved through.

To serve, place spoonfuls of mascarpone mixture and rhubarb in a bowl. Top with large shards of meringue to make a tower shape.

Process of making meringue

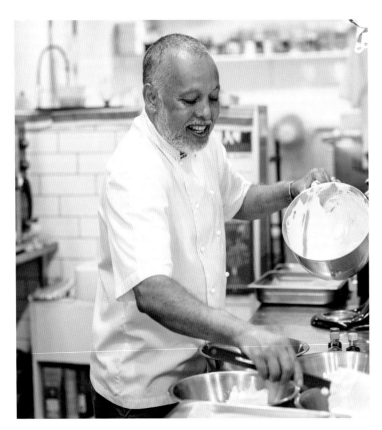

Room temperature raspberry soufflé

Serves: 10
Time: 1 hour, plus cooling time

5 egg whites
250 g (9 oz) sugar
500 ml (17 fl oz/2 cups) cream
350 g (12 oz) frozen raspberries
5 egg yolks
35 ml (1 fl oz) lemon juice
4 gelatin leaves
red or pink food coloring

Whisk the egg whites with 35 g (1 ¼ oz) of the sugar.

Whisk the cream with 35 g (1 ¼ oz) of the sugar.

Heat 180 g (6 ½ oz) of the sugar with 250 g (9 oz) of the raspberries in a saucepan over medium heat until the sugar is dissolved. Whisk the mixture into the egg yolks with the lemon juice.

Cook over a bain marie until slightly thickened. Add the gelatin and food coloring.

Allow the mixture to cool slightly over an ice bath, then whisk half the mixture into the egg whites and cream.

Fold the remaining mixture in gently, then add the remaining raspberries. Pour into molds and set in fridge.

To prepare the molds, use a dariole mold or ramekin, add a collar of doubled up foil and secure with rubber band.

To serve, remove the foil from the soufflé just before serving. Serve immediately at room temperature.

Rosemary & Cointreau brûlée

Serves: 6–8
Time: 2 hours, plus cooling time

½ bunch rosemary
750 ml (26 fl oz/3 cups) cream
2 tablespoons Cointreau
8 egg yolks
100 g (3 ½ oz) sugar
icing (confectioners') sugar, to dust
raspberries, to garnish (optional)

———————

Bruise the rosemary and add to a saucepan over low heat with the cream and Cointreau. Heat until small bubbles form at the edge.

Whisk the egg yolks and sugar together in a large bowl. Strain the hot cream into the yolk mixture and whisk until combined.

Preheat the oven to 160°C (315°F). Set coffee cups or molds in a deep, flat tray. Pour the mixture into the molds, leaving 5 mm (¼ inch) at the top. Add hot water to the tray (it should come halfway up the cups or molds).

Bake for 1 ½ hours. Remove the tray from the oven and allow molds sit in the tray for 15 minutes before removing to cool. Leave to cool completely before covering.

To serve, cover the brûlée with icing sugar and use a kitchen blow torch to caramelize. Dust with icing sugar.

Cinnamon-infused apple
& rhubarb crumble

Serves: 4–6
Time: 1 hour 10 minutes

125 g (4 ½ oz/1 cup) chopped rhubarb
2 cinnamon quills
100 g (3½ oz) brown sugar
¼ teaspoon Chinese five-spice
4 granny smith apples, peeled and diced
ice cream, to serve (optional)

Crumble

100 g (3 ½ oz) unsalted butter
50 g (1 ¾ oz) skim milk powder
50 g (1 ¾ oz) rolled oats
50 g (1 ¾ oz) brown sugar
50 g (1 ¾ oz) ground almonds
50 g (1 ¾ oz) plain (all-purpose) flour
¼ teaspoon ground cinnamon

In a saucepan over medium heat, place the rhubarb, cinnamon, brown sugar and five spice. Cook until the sugar dissolves and rhubarb starts to soften. Add the diced apples and cook for 10 minutes, or until just tender. Set aside.

Preheat the oven to 140°C (275°F). Line a baking tray with baking paper.

To make the crumble, combine the softened butter with milk powder, rolled oats, brown sugar, ground almonds, flour and cinnamon. Mix using your hands until crumbly. Spread on the baking tray and bake for 30 minutes, stirring around every 10 minutes. Set aside to cool.

Place the apple and rhubarb into individual ramekins and top with the crumble mixture. Bake at 180°C (350°F) for 10 minutes, or until golden brown.

Serve warm with ice cream, if desired.

Rosewater & saffron panna cotta
with poached pears

Serves: 4
Time: 1 hour, plus cooling

Panna cotta
375 ml (13 fl oz/1 ½ cups) cream
60 g (2 ¼ oz) sugar
1 teaspoon rosewater
a few threads of saffron
2 gelatin leaves
fresh mint, to garnish

Poached pears
250 ml (9 fl oz/1 cup) white wine
1 lemon, peel
2 cinnamon quills
2 star anise
a few saffron threads
400 g (14 oz) caster (superfine) sugar
4 pears, peeled

Heat the cream, sugar, rosewater and saffron in a saucepan over medium heat until boiling. Remove from the heat and strain into a bowl.

Bloom the gelatin leaves in cold water until softened. Remove and squeeze out any excess water before adding to the warm cream. Stir to dissolve.

Pour the mixture into four panna cotta molds and set aside to cool.

To make the poached pears, place all of the ingredients, except the pears, in a saucepan. Bring to the boil, then reduce the heat to very low. Add the pears and add 1 litre (35 fl oz/4 cups) of water, making sure there is enough liquid to cover the pears. Place a cartouche of baking paper on top of the pears and cook slowly for about 1 hour until tender. Remove from the heat and allow the pears cool in the syrup.

Unmold the panna cotta by dipping the molds into warm water. Run a paring knife around the top edge and turn over into your hand until the panna cotta is released from the mold. Place on a plate and remove any excess water. Place whole or sliced pear as desired next to the panna cotta. Garnish with sesame tuiles and fresh mint leaves.

Halawa marquise
with sesame seed crisps

Serves: 6–8
Time: 6 hours

4 gelatin leaves, titanium
100 ml (3 ½ fl oz) cream
100 g (3 ½ oz) sugar
500 g (1 lb 2 oz) halawa
500 g (1 lb 2 oz) plain or Greek-style
yoghurt
1 teaspoon rosewater
pistachio powder
edible flowers, to garnish

Pistachio anglaise
4 egg yolks
50 g (1 ¾ oz) sugar
200 ml (7 fl oz) cream
1 tablespoon pistachio paste
sesame crisps (see p153)

Soak the gelatin in 500 ml (17 fl oz/2 cups) ice water.

Place the cream and sugar in a saucepan over medium heat and bring to the boil.

Crush the halawa in a large bowl, then add the yoghurt and mix until combined.

Add drained gelatin to the hot cream, whisk well to combine. Strain the gelatin mix into the yoghurt, add rosewater and mix with electric beaters until combined.

Pour into a flat tray about 18 x 30 cm (7 x 12 in). Set aside for at least 4 hours to cool and set.

To make the pistachio anglaise, mix the egg yolks and sugar in a bowl. Heat the cream in a saucepan over medium heat. Whisk the egg yolks over a bain marie until warm. Add the pistachio paste and heated cream and keep whisking over the bain marie until mixture is thick enough to coat the back of a spoon. Allow to cool.

To serve, cut large squares from the set marquise and place on the center of the plate. Drizzle anglaise around the marquise and place pieces of the sesame crisp on the edge. Dust with pistachio powder and garnish with edible flowers.

Organic chia pudding
with summer fruits

Serves: 12
Time: 30 minutes

1 litre (35 fl oz/4 cups) coconut cream

150 g (5 ½ oz) caster (superfine) sugar

250 g (9 oz) chia seeds

100 g (3 ½ oz) raspberries

100 g (3 ½ oz) blueberries

50 g (1 ¾ oz) strawberries

150 g (5 ½ oz) mango, sliced and diced

1 teaspoon olive oil

1 teaspoon sugar syrup

zest of 1 lime

nasturtium leaves, to garnish

edible flowers, to garnish

1 tablespoon roasted coconut chips

Bring the coconut cream and sugar to the boil, then remove from the heat.

Add the chia seeds and stir constantly until slightly cooled and thickened.

Spoon into martini glasses filling to halfway and store in the fridge.
(They will keep for a couple of days.)

Mix the fruit gently with the olive oil, sugar syrup and lime zest.

To serve, top the chia pudding with some of the fruit and garnish with nasturtium leaves, coconut chips and edible flowers.

Almond & prune sticky date pudding with butterscotch sauce

Serves: 8
Time: 1½ hours

150 g (5 ½ oz) dates
100 g (3 ½ oz) prunes
1 teaspoon bicarbonate of soda (baking soda)
60 g (2 ¼ oz) unsalted butter
250 g (9 oz) sugar
5 eggs
200 g (7 oz) ground almonds
200 g (7 oz) self-raising (self-rising) flour
strawberries and vanilla ice cream, to serve (optional)

Butterscotch sauce
250 g (9 oz) butter
250 g (9 oz) dark brown sugar
500 ml (17 fl oz/2 cups) double cream

Preheat the oven to 160°C (315°F). Lightly grease a 23 cm (9 in) cake tin and line with baking paper.

Place the dates, prunes and 250 ml (9 fl oz/1 cup) water in a saucepan. Bring to the boil and simmer for 10 minutes, or until soft. Remove from the heat. Add the bicarbonate of soda and mix through well to soften the fruit. Set aside until needed.

Cream the butter and sugar in an electric mixer. Add the eggs one at a time, beating well after each addition. Fold through the ground almonds and flour. Fold through the date and prune mixture. Transfer the mixture into the prepared tin and bake for 45 minutes to 1 hour. Allow to cool.

To make the butterscotch sauce, beat the butter and sugar in a saucepan over low heat until the sugar dissolves. Increase the heat to medium and cook until it starts to bubble. Stir continually and cook for a further few minutes. In a separate saucepan, heat the cream until almost boiling, then add to the butter and sugar, taking care as it may splash.

To serve, cut circles from the pudding with a ring mold. Heat for a few minutes in a steam oven or microwave to warm. Pour the butterscotch sauce over the puddings. Serve with strawberries and vanilla ice-cream if desired.

Flourless chocolate cake

Serves: 8
Time: 1 ½ hours

300 g (10 ½ oz) chocolate
250 g (9 oz) unsalted butter
7 eggs
200 g (7 oz) sugar
300 g (10 ½ oz) ground almonds
almond macarons and strawberry (to
garnish, optional)

Chocolate sauce

300 g (10 oz) dark chocolate
150 ml (5 fl oz) boiling water

Preheat the oven to 180°C (350°F). Lightly grease a 23 cm (9 in) cake tin and line with baking paper.

Melt the chocolate and butter over a bain marie.

In a separate bowl, whisk the eggs and sugar until pale and the sugar is dissolved.

Fold the ground almonds into the egg mixture. Fold the melted chocolate and butter through.

Fold the mixture into the prepared tin. Place the tin in a water bath and bake for 45 minutes to 1 hour.

Place a chopping board on top of the cake tin and flip it over before gently removing tin. Let it cool for 15 minutes, then transfer to a cake cooling rack to cool completely.

To make sauce, combine boiling water and chocolate and whisk until smooth.

To serve, slice cake and place on the center of the plate. Drizzle sauce over cake and garnish with almond macaroons and strawberry (optional).

Chapter 5

BASICS

Vegetable stock

Makes: 3-4 litres (102–135 fl oz/12–16 cups)
Time: 1 hour

2 large onion, diced
4 large carrots, diced
6 celery sticks, diced
1 fennel bulb, diced
1 handful parsley stalks
4 bay leaves
1 teaspoon peppercorns, whole

Add all of the ingredients to a large stockpot with 3.5 litres (118 fl oz/14 cups) of water. Bring to the boil, then reduce the heat and simmer for about 30 minutes, remove any scum that floats to the surface.

Remove from the heat. Strain and retain the stock, discard the vegetables.

Store in a sealed container and keep in fridge for 2-3 days or freezer for up to 2 months.

Fish stock

Makes: 4 litres (135 fl oz/16 cups)
Time: 1 hour

2 onions, finely diced
2 celery sticks, finely diced
1 leek, finely diced
2 carrots, finely diced
1 bunch dill stems
zest of 1 lemon
2 snapper heads
4 litres (135 fl oz/16 cups) water

Wash the fish heads in cold water.

Add all of the ingredients to a large stockpot. Bring to the boil, then reduce the heat to low and simmer for 35 minutes. Remove any scum that floats to the surface.

Remove from the heat and strain. Retain the stock and discard the vegetables and fish heads.

Store in sealed container and keep in fridge for 2-3 days or freezer for up to 2 months.

Seafood stock

Makes: 3 litres
Time: 45 minutes

1 kg (2 lb 4 oz) mussels

1 kg (2 lb 4 oz) vongole or clams

500 g (1 lb 2 oz) prawn (shrimp) heads

2 onions (roughly chopped)

8 garlic cloves, crushed

750 ml (26 fl oz/3 cups) white wine

2 large onions, finely diced

1 leek, finely diced

6 celery sticks, finely diced

100 g (3 ½ oz) butter

4 fish heads, snapper or barramundi

1 lemon, peeled 1 fennel bulb

1 bunch dill

Wash the mussels, vongole and prawn heads to remove any grit.

In a large pot over medium heat, sauté the chopped onion and garlic until soft, then add the white wine.

Add the mussels, vongole and prawns and steam for 10 minutes, then set aside.

Add the diced onion, leek and celery to a large pot and sauté in the butter until soft.

Add 3 litres (102 fl oz/12 cups) of water and the fish heads and simmer for 25 minutes. Remove any scum that floats to the surface. Add lemon, fennel and dill. After 25 minutes, add in the mussel stock and cook for a further few minutes. Remove from the heat and strain through muslin for a clear broth.

Store in sealed container and keep in fridge for 2-3 days or freezer for up to 2 months.

Aromatic brown chicken stock

Makes: 3 litres (102 fl oz/12 cups)
Time: 2 hours

2 kg (4 lb 8 oz) chicken carcass, organic or free range
3 kg (6 lb 12 oz) chicken wings
2 large onions, diced
4 large carrots, diced
6 celery sticks, diced
2 litres (70 fl oz/8 cups) sherry
10 garlic cloves
100 g (3 ½ oz) ginger
1 bunch thyme
3 cinnamon quills
3 star anise
100 g (3 ½ oz) butter
200 g (7 oz) tomato paste (concentrated purée)

Preheat the oven to 180°C (350°F).

Place the chicken carcasses and wings on a baking tray. Roast for 45 minutes, or until golden brown.

Mix the diced onions, carrots and celery with the butter and tomato paste, place on another baking tray and roast for 45 minutes, or until browned, stirring occasionally for an even color.

In a large stockpot, add the chicken and roasted vegetables.

Deglaze the roasting pans with sherry. Add to the pot with the remaining herbs, spices and 2 litres (70 fl oz/8 cups) of water. Bring to the boil and simmer for 45 minutes, removing any scum that comes to the surface periodically. Strain the stock and discard the chicken and vegetables.

Store in sealed container and keep in fridge for 2-3 days or freezer for up to 2 months.

Chicken stock

Makes: 3 litres (102 fl oz/12 cups)
Time: 1½ hours

2 kg (4 lb 8 oz) chicken carcasses
3 kg (6 lb 12 oz) chicken wings
2 large onions, diced
4 large carrots, diced
6 celery sticks, diced
1 bunch thyme
1 handful parsley stalks
1 garlic clove, halved
4 bay leaves
1 tablespoon whole peppercorn

Add all of the ingredients to a large stockpot along with 3.5 litres (118 fl oz/14 cups) of water. Bring to the boil, then reduce the heat and simmer for 45 minutes. Remove any scum that rises to the surface periodically.

Strain the stock and discard the chicken, herbs and vegetables.

Store in sealed container and keep in fridge for 2-3 days or freezer for up to 2 months.

Beef stock

Makes: 2 litres (70 fl oz/8 cups)
Time: 6 hours

4 kg (9 lb) beef bones, with marrow
1 pig's trotter
4 large onions, diced
4 large carrots, diced
6 celery sticks, diced
2 leeks, diced
1 tablespoon juniper berries
2 tablespoons peppercorns
100 g (3 ½ oz) ginger, roughly chopped
100 g (3 ½ oz) whole peeled garlic cloves
6 bay leaves
250 g (9 oz/1 cup) tomato paste
(concentrated purée)
2 x 750 ml (26 fl oz) bottles red wine, such
as cabernet sauvignon
1 cup goji berries

Preheat the oven to 180°C (350°F).

Add the bones and trotter to a large roasting pan. Roast for 45 minutes.

Add the diced vegetables to the roasted bones with the juniper berries, peppercorns, ginger, garlic, bay leaves and tomato paste. Roast the meat and vegetables for a further 45 minutes. Transfer the meat and vegetables to a very large stockpot.

Deglaze the roasting tray with some of the wine and add this to the pot along with the goji berries and 6 litres (203 fl oz/24 cups) of water. Bring to the boil, then reduce the heat to very low and simmer for 4–5 hours, adding more water if necessary. Remove any scum that floats to the surface periodically. Strain the stock and add back into the pot. Cook until reduced by about three-quarters.

Store in sealed container and keep in fridge for 2-3 days or freezer for up to 2 months.

Lamb stock

Makes: 2 litres (70 fl oz/8 cups)
Time: 7 hours

4 onions, diced
4 celery sticks, diced
1 leek, diced
4 carrot, diced
5 kg (10 lb 4 oz) lamb bones, with marrow
250 g (9 oz/1 cup) tomato paste
(concentrated purée)
6 bay leaves
2 teaspoons peppercorns
2 x 750 ml (26 fl oz) bottles red wine, such
as cabernet sauvignon
1 bunch rosemary
One head of garlic, cut in half

Preheat the oven to 180°C (350°F).

Put the diced vegetables in a large roasting pan
with the lamb bones and tomato paste. Roast
for 20–30 minutes until golden.

Place the roasted bones and vegetables in a
large stockpot with the bay leaves, peppercorns
and 6 litres (203 fl oz/24 cups) of water. Bring
to the boil, then reduce the heat to low and
simmer for 4 hours.

Strain, then return the stock to the pot with
the red wine, rosemary and garlic. Simmer for
a further 2 hours.

Store in sealed container and keep in fridge for
2-3 days or freezer for up to 2 months.

Ras el Hanout

Makes: 800 g (1 lb 12 oz)
Time: 10 minutes

50 g (1¾ oz) whole black peppercorns
50 g (1¾ oz) whole cumin seeds
50 g (1¾ oz) cinnamon quills
50 g (1¾ oz) whole star anise
50 g (1¾ oz) cardamom pods
50 g (1¾ oz) ground ginger
50 g (1¾ oz) whole cloves
50 g (1¾ oz) ground sweet paprika
50 g (1¾ oz) oregano powder
50 g (1¾ oz) thyme powder
50 g (1¾ oz) sumac powder
50 g (1¾ oz) whole white peppercorns
50 g (1¾ oz) dried rose petals
50 g (1¾ oz) dried black lemon
50 g (1¾ oz) whole black cardamom
50 g (1¾ oz) grated nutmeg

Toast all of the whole spices in a dry, non-stick frying pan until fragrant. Allow to cool, then blend in a spice grinder or mortar and pestle until finely ground. Shift any large pieces and regrind with the remaining spices.

Mix all of the spices together. Store in airtight container for up to 2 months.

Note: Recommended for stews and grilled meat or chicken.

Coya spice blend

Makes: 500 g (1 lb 2 oz)
Time: 5 minutes

100 g (3 ½ oz) onion powder
100 g (3 ½ oz) garlic powder
100 g (3 ½ oz) fennel powder
100 g (3 ½ oz) white pepper
100 g (3 ½ oz) celery salt

Mix all of the ingredients together and store in an airtight container for up to 2 months.

Note: Recommended for grilled fish and grilled chicken breast. It can also be used as a rub for short ribs. Rub into the meat, wrap in foil with a little white wine and cook until tender.

Baharat

Makes: 700 g (1 lb 9 oz)
Time: 15 minutes

100 g (3 ½ oz) black peppercorn
100 g (3 ½ oz) cumin seeds
100 g (3 ½ oz) cinnamon quills
100 g (3 ½ oz) star anise
100 g (3 ½ oz) cardamom pods
100 g (3 ½ oz) cloves
100 g (3 ½ oz) ground ginger

Toast the peppercorns in a dry, non-stick frying pan until fragrant, then place in a spice grinder or mortar and pestle.

Continue toasting each ingredient (except for ground ginger), separately for best results.

Grind all the ingredients to a fine powder. Store in an airtight container for up to 15 days.

Note: Baharat is recommended as a seasoning for chicken, lamb or beef.

Moroccan spice, Tagine spice mix

Makes: 200 g (7 oz)
Time: 10 minutes

50 g (1 ¾ oz) cumin seeds
50 g (1 ¾ oz) coriander seeds
50 g (1 ¾ oz) cassia bark
20 g (¾ oz) ground turmeric
20 g (¾ oz) sweet paprika
a few threads of saffron
2 teaspoons lemon zest

Break the cassia bark into small pieces and add to a dry, non-stick frying pan with the coriander seeds and cumin seeds. Toast over medium heat until fragrant, then remove from the heat and cool.

When cool, place in a spice grinder and blend. Alternatively, you can crush them with a mortar and pestle, then strain out any large pieces that remain.

Add the turmeric, sweet paprika, saffron and lemon zest and mix well. Store in an airtight container for up to 15 days.

Garlic aïoli

Makes: 1.5 litres (52 fl oz/6 cups)
Time: 1 hour

1 whole head garlic
5 egg yolks
175 ml (5 ½ fl oz/2/3 cup) white vinegar
1 tablespoon dijon mustard
1 litre (35 fl oz/4 cups) vegetable oil
250 ml (9 fl oz/1 cup) olive oil
salt and pepper, to season

Wrap the garlic in foil and roast in a 180°C (350°F) oven for 15 minutes, or until softened.

Place the egg yolks, vinegar and mustard in a bowl and over a double boiler, whisk constantly until eggs are slightly cooked. They will become pale and thickened.

Place the mixture in a blender. Squeeze the softened garlic into the blender, blend and then drizzle the oils in very slowly so aïoli doesn't split. When all the oil is added it will become thick and increase in volume. Season to taste.

Note: Discard any unused aïoli on the day it is made.

Lime aïoli

Makes: 1.5 litres (52 fl oz/6 cups)
Time: 30 minutes

5 egg yolks
175 ml (5 ½ fl oz/2/3 cup) lime juice
2 tablespoons white vinegar
1 tablespoon dijon mustard
1 litre (35 fl oz/4 cups) vegetable oil
250 ml (9 fl oz/1 cup) olive oil
zest of 1 lime
salt and pepper, to season

Place the egg yolks, lime juice, vinegar and mustard in a bowl and over a double boiler, whisk constantly until eggs are slightly cooked. They will become pale and thickened.

Place the mixture in a blender and drizzle the oils in very slowly so the aïoli doesn't split. When all the oil is added it will become thick and increase in volume.

Add the lime zest and season to taste.

Note: Discard any unused aïoli on the day it is made.

Green tomato & chili jam paste

Makes: 750 g (26 ½ oz)
Time: 30 minutes

250 ml (9 fl oz/1 cup) white wine
125 ml (4 ½ fl oz/½ cup) white vinegar
200 g (7 oz) sugar
1 cinnamon sticks
1 star anise
5 bay leaves
2 red chilies, cut in halves
1 kg (2 lb 4 oz) green tomatoes, diced

In a heavy-based pan over medium heat, reduce the white wine, vinegar, sugar, cinnamon, star anise and bay leaves.

Add the chili and boil for 10 minutes, then add the green tomato and cook until soft.

Serve with pork, chicken or fish.

Gourmet bread

Makes: 1 tray
Time: 2 hours

1 kg (2 lb 4 oz) baker's flour
12 g (¼ oz) dry yeast
12 g (¼ oz) baking powder
¼ teaspoon sugar
sea salt
fresh or dried herbs, to taste
cracked black pepper, to taste
olive oil
olives, artichokes (optional)

Line a greased tray with baking paper and coat lightly with olive oil.

Mix together the flour, yeast, baking powder, sugar, pinch of salt, herbs and pepper and in a large bowl. Add cold water slowly and mix until a thick cake mixture consistency. Mix through your flavorings, if required.

Scoop the mix into a prepared tray and flatten out with olive oil coated hands. Sprinkle with salt, pepper and herbs. Leave to prove in a warm place for 1 hour.

Preheat the oven to 240°C (475°F).

Bake for about 50 minutes, or until golden.

Sesame seed crisps

Makes: 1 kg (2 lb 4 oz)
Time: 30 minutes

500 g (1 lb 2 oz) sugar
500 ml (17 fl oz) water
200 g (7 oz) white sesame seeds
50 g (1 ¾ oz) black sesame seeds

Preheat the oven to 120°C (235°F). Line a baking tray with a silicone mat.

Heat the sugar and 500 ml (17 fl oz/2 cups) of water in a saucepan until the sugar is dissolved.

Mix the sesame seeds into the sugar syrup, then spread onto the baking tray.

Bake for 10–15 minutes, or until golden. Leave to cool on the tray until crisp, then break into shards. Store in an airtight container.

Coral tuiles

Serves: 5
Time: 30 minutes

10 g (¼ oz) plain (all-purpose) flour
30 g (1 oz) vegetable oil
10 g (¼ oz) coloring or squid ink
80 ml (2 ½ fl oz) water

Put all of the ingredients and 80 ml (2 ½ fl oz) of water in a bowl and whisk until combined. Pour into a squeeze bottle.

Heat a small frying pan over high heat. Squeeze the tuile mix into the pan in a fine layer. When it starts to sizzle, turn the heat all the way down (very low). Cook for 5 minutes, or until crisp. Remove from the pan and place on a wire rack to drain the oil.

To serve, use as a garnish for entrée, main and dessert dishes.

Sesame seed tuiles

Serves: 10 as a dessert garnish
Time: 1 hour 30 minutes

100 g (3½ oz) simple syrup
10 g (¼ oz) honey
25 g (1 oz) black sesame seeds
25 g (1 oz) white sesame seeds

Preheat the oven to 170°C (325°F).

Line a baking tray with baking paper.

Combine all of the ingredients and spread flat on the baking tray.

Bake for 10–12 minutes, then remove from the oven and cool until crisp. Break into pieces and serve with dessert.

Simple syrup

Makes: 1 litre
Time: 15 minutes

460 g (1 lb/2 cups) caster (superfine) sugar
750 ml (26 fl oz/3 cups) water

Put all of the ingredients in a saucepan and heat until sugar is dissolved. Store for later use.

Store in the fridge for up to 3 months.

Acknowledgements

I first stepped into the kitchen when I was twelve. I followed my mother around the markets, the tastes of those markets were never far from my memory. During the school holidays other kids would play in the yard, but I loved spending time with my mum in the kitchen, learning spices and herbs. It was the food of my childhood, one of the joys of my rich cultural heritage. It is the food that I have always loved most, that I have taken with me wherever I go.

Food and stories have always inspire me, listened to my mum's stories and my partner's tale about her experience with food was just fascinating! We all have different ideas, sharing and exchanging ideas is the most wonderful thing when it comes to cooking. *COYA* is all about family and friends, food that can be cooked together, shared together. Always sharing, always giving. After all, food does bring people together.

In this book, I emphasise herbs and spices that are used in the Middle Eastern cuisine and sharing my French cooking techniques that I've learnt while I was in Europe. Each recipe plays a special part in celebrating and maintaining my rich cultural traditions.

I dedicate this book to the memory of my mother and mother-in-law. My dream came true with my partner's support and encouragement, also inspiration from my boys, Joshua & Jovani.

156

Index

First published in 2019 by New Holland Publishers
London • Sydney • Auckland

Bentinck House, 3–8 Bolsover Street, London W1W 6AB, UK
1/66 Gibbes Street, Chatswood, NSW 2067, Australia
5/39 Woodside Ave, Northcote, Auckland 0627, New Zealand

newhollandpublishers.com

A record of this book is held at the British Library and the National Library of Australia.

ISBN   9781921024863

Group Managing Director: Fiona Schultz
Project Editor: Elise James
Designer: Yolanda La Gorcé
Production Director: Arlene Gippert
Photographer: Rebecca Elliott
Stylist: Tom Miles
Printer: Toppan Leefung Printing Limited

10 9 8 7 6 5 4 3 2 1

Keep up with New Holland Publishers on Facebook
facebook.com/NewHollandPublishers